D1286663

SUN, SAND, AND STEEL

Costumes and Equipment of the Spanish-Mexican Southwest

This is a book about the Spanish and Mexican people who explored and settled much of the Southwest from Texas to California — how they dressed and something of the everyday tools they used.

Much information in this book came from examining actual historical costumes and equipment. Whenever possible, drawings and paintings made at the time the costumes were worn have been reproduced or carefully redrawn for clarity and emphasis. Information from records and documents written at the time have also been included in the text.

Sun,

Silver saddle ornament of the 1500's includes lion with crown from the royal Spanish crest.

Sand, and Steel

Costumes and
Equipment of the
Spanish-Mexican Southwest
Written and Illustrated
by GLEN DINES

G. P. Putnam's Sons
New York

CONTENTS

ACKNOWLEDGMENTS

The author extends his gratitude to the many librarians who were helpful in researching this book and especially the staff of the Bancroft Library, University of California, Berkeley, California; Edwin Carter, De Young Museum of Art, San Francisco, California; Pierce Chamberlin, Arizona Pioneer Society Museum, Tucson, Arizona; Chuck Daily, Museum of New Mexico, Palace of Governors, Santa Fe, New Mexico; John MacKenzie, La Purisma Mission State Historical Park, Lompoc, California; Luis Martinez, Tubac State Park Museum, Tubac, Arizona; and to the staffs of the Los Angeles County Museum of Natural History, Los Angeles, California, and the Thomas Gilcrease Institute of American History and Art, Tulsa, Oklahoma. Special thanks to Rickie, Lisa, and Woody, who shared the rigors of early spring travel in the Southwest.

SUN, SAND, AND STEEL

Costumes and Equipment of the Spanish-Mexican Southwest

1. SWORD AND SAIL

First there was the sun and beneath the sun the land — vast and windswept. From the north came people — hunters and planters, men and women — earth-colored. They shared the land with the animals and wind. For a thousand years, ten thousand years, one hundred thousand years, the earth and the earth-colored people lived as one under the golden sun.

Then strange bearded men came riding out of the south. They did not come to share the land but to explore and

conquer. And even the glorious sun was forced to dance on the keen edges of their steel swords.

These early Spanish explorers did not gallop about the New World dressed in fancy, high-combed helmets, shiny breastplates, and thick-soled high-top boots. Certainly not the saddle-weary band who plodded into present-day Arizona on a hot summer day in 1540.

Only a few could afford metal armor. High-combed morion helmets were not worn much before 1560 and boots with heels and soles did not come into fashion until after 1600.

Nor were the men who explored the Southwest with Fráncisco Vásquez de Coronado or Juan de Oñate part of an army. They were a collection of armed civilians who had agreed to follow orders . . . more or less. These early explorers wore the basic men's dress of the day, as shown at the left: underdrawers, shirt (A), and tight-fitting one-piece hose (B) fitted with a flap (C) called a codpiece. The hose was often cut full and "pouched" at the top, as indicated by the dashed lines. Most of the shirts and hose worn on expeditions were cotton or wool. However, the few men who could afford several pack animals carried hose of linen and silk and elegantly trimmed and embroidered wardrobes of satin and velvet into the harsh desert wilderness.

A doublet (below, left) was usually worn over the shirt and the hose fastened to it by ties of cloth or leather called points. A jerkin, often sleeveless (below, right), fit over the doublet. Until the 1600's, separate stockings of wool or soft buckskin were sometimes worn over the hose for added protection and warmth.

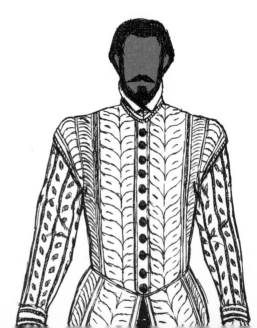

Light, heelless shoes, sometimes slit and decorated, and small cloth hats and cloaks or short capes completed the dress.

Below: (A) Typical 1540 man's costume: shirt with high neck and turn-down collar; jerkin with sleeves puffed to elbow. (B) 1560 — bulblike "trunk-hose" stuffed with horse hair; short Spanish cape. (C) 1600 — knee-length breeches; doublet with pointed "peasecod" waist; separate stockings replacing hose.

A   B   C

Fig. 1

Fig. 2

If one garment could be called typical of the early Spanish explorations, it was probably the padded jerkin of cloth or leather. Long worn in Europe, this inexpensive armor appears in drawings made by Indians of Mexico in the 1550's (Figures 1–2). The Aztec warriors who fought the Spanish also used padded armor, as shown in Figure 3, from a 1550 drawing. The Spanish were quick to adopt this light, easy-to-wear protection. Members of Hernando de Soto's 1540 expedition in Florida wore canvas coats stuffed with cotton. In 1560, French explorers in Florida also wore padded jerkins, as pictured in Plate 1. Costumes in this beautifully detailed illustration are of a later date, however, since the engraving was not made until 1588.

Spanish explorers in the Southwest preferred leather. A careful listing of the equipment of Coronado's expedition reveals buckskin jackets as the most popular form of armor. Most of Oñate's company wore jackets of leather — possibly a combination of the sleeveless jerkin and the longer, Aztec cotton armor — a garment destined to become famous throughout the Southwest.

Fig. 3

Plate 1

Fig. 4

Fig. 5

Fig. 6

When not fighting or otherwise impressing the natives, the explorers dressed in the same traveling costume they would have worn in Spain. Figure 4, from a drawing by an Indian artist in Mexico, shows a Spaniard of the early 1500's in riding costume: soft hat, short cloak or cape, soft leather riding boots with no heels and pointed spurs. Figure 5 is from a 1529 drawing by a German artist in Spain. From hat to spurs, the costumes are almost identical. Another example of similar styles in Spain and the New World are the short capes with hanging sleeves and the ruffled shirt collars which appear in Figure 6, from an engraving by a Flemish artist of the late 1500's, and Figure 7, from a drawing by a Mexican Indian of the 1550's. The cruel punishment shown in Figure 7 was evidently common, since it appears in other drawings of the time. Another interesting detail is the Spaniard's spurs. The round, star-shaped rowels are a change from the older, pointed style.

Fig. 7

13

Plate 2

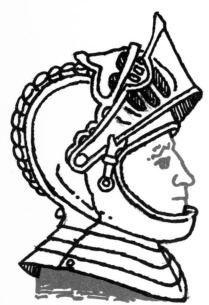

Fig. 8

Civilians or not, the Spanish who came to the New World were willing and able to fight. The drawing above, done by a Mexican artist, shows this fierce spirit better than words can tell. It also reveals some interesting details of Spanish mid-1500 arms and armor.

The famous conquistador Hernando Cortez (A) wears several pieces of plate armor, including breastplates, pauldron on the shoulders, and vambraces on upper and lower arms. To his right stands one of his captains (B) in "half armor." He holds a round shield called a target and wears a closed helmet with movable face guard. Figure 8, taken from a Spanish tapestry of the 1540's, shows this same type of helmet with a latch holding up the face guard.

The best suits of armor were masterpieces of metalcraft, carefully fitted and handsomely decorated. Such suits were very expensive, however, and carried only by the leaders and wealthy members of an expedition.

In the description of equipment carried by 292 men who marched with Coronado, only two complete sets of armor are listed. Second to leather jackets, old-fashioned chain mail was the most popular armor. Many men wore both leather jackets and coats of mail of various lengths and styles. All the early explorers wore some kind of helmet and some wore odd pieces of plate armor.

Below: Spanish explorer wearing popular Burgonet helmet. Right: Typical suit of armor of mid-1500's. Parts in gray are most frequently listed in records of early expeditions. Detail shows construction of chain mail.

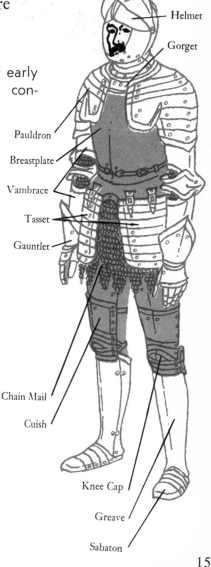

Helmet

Gorget

Pauldron

Breastplate

Vambrace

Tasset

Gauntlet

Chain Mail

Cuish

Knee Cap

Greave

Sabaton

15

Fig. 9

In the 1500's, most men carried a dagger and the will to use it. A gentleman's dress included a rapier as well. For the Spaniard on horseback, the lance was a favorite — and fearsome — weapon. Long-handled, axlike halberds were often carried as a mark of rank by sergeants. Captains used shorter spearlike partisans (Figure 9B). These weapons remained much the same in the 1500's. What changed was the use of firearms. In 1524 an entire company of crossbowmen marched with Cortez. Twenty years later Coronado's records list 21 crossbows and 25 harquebuses — probably smoothbore, muzzle-loading matchlocks, as shown above. Coronado also brought along some small brass cannon. In 1597 Oñate's expedition included many firearms — not one crossbow. Figure 9, taken from a 1588 engraving, shows method of carrying dagger (A). Equipment of harquebusier includes fuselike match (C), made of loosely braided cord soaked in saltpeter solution and powder flask (D).

Above: Harquebuse with cumbersome matchlock firing mechanism. Lighted match ready to be triggered into firing position indicated by dash lines. By 1600, more efficient wheel lock mechanism (left) was replacing matchlocks.

A halberd with four-foot handle, similar to those pictured in Plate 1, page 14. Above the halberd is a rapier with a matching dagger, typical of types used during middle 1500's.

17

Fig. 10

While Spanish explorers trudged across dusty deserts, Spanish sailors struggled northward along a wilderness Pacific shore. Many of their leaky little ships were built in primitive Mexican shipyards — a poor match for contrary ocean currents and head winds. Disease and sudden storms were constant companions. But if the going was rugged and dangerous, travel aboard ship allowed many of the fineries which land travelers could not carry. Sea captain Hernando de Alarcón, who sailed the western shore of Mexico while Coronado marched inland, carried many changes of clothes and enjoyed his scanty meals served on silver dishes.

Common seamen of the early 1500's were already wearing the ankle-length trousers which would become their trademark in years to come (see Figure 10, from a 1529 drawing). Sailors also wore easy-to-roll pantaloons long before these baggy trousers came into style. A seaman of 1581 (Figure 11) wears pantaloons, fur-trimmed cloak, and tall, close-fitting cap — all popular apparel for sailors. Figure 12, taken from a drawing of the 1590's, shows a Danish seaman wearing a fur cap and wielding a halberd much like those carried by Cortez's men forty years before.

Fig. 11

Fig. 12

Crewman (A), surveying California coast in early 1600's, wears loose-fitting tunic and trousers. Ship's captain (B) is dressed in doublet, leather jerkin, and baggy pants of the period. Armor of harquebusier (C) includes morion helmet and brigandine (canvas jacket lined with metal plates.) Officer (D) wears half armor.

A

Spanish explorers of late 1500's prepare to skirmish with Southwest Indians. (A) Mounted officer, in full armor, dons plumed closed helmet. Attendant holds lance and

B

double oval-shaped shield called *adarga*. (B) Horseman dressed in soft hat, short Spanish cape, doublet, jerkin, hose, and soft leather boots. (C) Sergeant with halberd

C

D

E

wears helmet and padded jerkin.
Shoulder sash also indicates rank.
(D) Harquebusier wears helmet,
leather jacket, coat of mail, thigh
and knee guards. (E) Horseman,

with Burgonet helmet and separate face guard, called *bevor*, carries round steel target. His horse
wears leather armor. Dogs were
often taken on expeditions.

2. LANCE AND CROSS

 The bearded conquistadores moved across the land looking for gold and glory. Finding neither, they marched away.

 Then from the south came Spanish lancers riding in the name of their king. They looked at the land, but only as a place to build forts against the coming of other soldiers of other kings. With the proud lancers came humble priests. But even these barefoot brothers did not see the land. Instead, they saw the earth-colored people and a rich harvest of souls for their God.

And one day the morning sun, sliding across the land, stumbled on the edge of a thick-walled church-fort.

In the 1600's men's dress in New Spain followed the fashion styles of Europe. Somber-colored tight-fitting suits gave way to showy "Three Musketeer" outfits with flounces of lace and ribbon and floppy-topped high-heeled boots. Linen shirt, a waistcoat (forerunner of the present-day vest) drawn up tightly at the waist, and knee-length breeches became the basic items of dress. The most fashionable waistcoats were

Neckcloth
Coat
Waistcoat

Breeches

made of embroidered satin. Knitted stockings of cotton, wool, or silk and shoes with heels and buckles or bows completed the typical wardrobe of the late 1600's, as shown at the left.

Changes in men's fashions from 1650 up to the 1800's are pictured below. Waistcoats and outer full-skirted frock coats were gradually shortened and trimmed. The huge periwigs shrunk to small powdered wigs and finally disappeared altogether. Full-length, tight-fitting trousers appeared and tall hats made of felt or beaver pelts became fashionable. However, fashion changes were slow to reach the remote Southwest frontier and fancy fashion extremes were rarely seen. The everyday dress in the mid-1700's was probably much like the costume in Figure 13, taken from an early drawing of the famous Presidio of San Francisco, California. And everywhere on the frontier definite Spanish touches were to be seen.

1650   1750   1800

Fig. 13

A well-to-do ranchero of the late 1780's is pictured at the right. His wardrobe includes (A) broad-brimmed hat trimmed under the brim with silver or gold thread, (B) kerchief tied around his head, (C) short bolero jacket of velvet, (D) an ankle-length cloak of broadcloth, and (E) a brightly colored waist sash of silk. His breeches are of satin. On his feet he wears ornamented, slipperlike shoes of dyed deerskin. The soles are turned up slightly at the toes to prevent the shoes from rubbing against the stirrup covers.

Men also wore sandals made of leather strips fastened across the toes, instep, and heel. Sometimes the feet were wrapped in red cloth which showed between the strips.

But the two most famous costumes of the frontier — those of the priests and soldiers — were worn over the everyday clothing and remained virtually the same throughout the Spanish-Mexican period.

JESUIT   DOMINICAN   FRANCISCAN

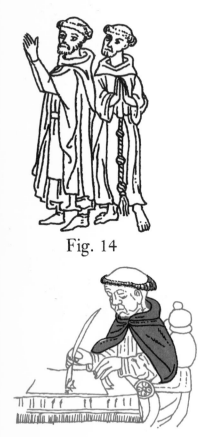

Fig. 14

Fig. 15

Priests of the Catholic Church sailed with Christopher Columbus, marched with Cortez, and rode beside Coronado. A good part of the exploration and settlement of the Southwest was done by members of three religious orders of this church: Franciscan, Dominican, and Jesuit. The official habits, or gowns, of these brotherhoods are pictured above. Made of coarse sackcloth, the habits worn by Franciscans and Dominicans were styled after the thirteenth-century dress of their founders, Saint Francis and Saint Dominio (see Figure 14, taken from an old woodcut). Dominican friars — brothers — wore a white tunic, a white apronlike scapulary, and a long black mantle. Figure 15, from a drawing made in Mexico in the 1540's, shows a Dominican friar with his head shaved on top to form a clerical tonsure. Franciscans wore simpler habits of gray, with a white cord worn around the waist and knotted at one end. Franciscan friars went barefoot or wore simple open-toed sandals.

Both Franciscans and Dominicans wore a separate capelike garment which fit over the shoulder with a hood to cover the head. The view of a Franciscan friar from a 1786 drawing made in California (Figure 17) shows this cowl, or capuche, very clearly.

The black robes of the Jesuits featured a high collar, shown in Figure 16, from a drawing of the early 1600's. This order was founded in 1534 by Ignatius of Loyola.

Life on the frontier was primitive, even for humble priests pledged to poverty. Habits, patched and repatched, became tattered and nondescript. Even the colors changed. One Franciscan had his threadbare habit unraveled and rewoven by Indians, only to learn that the one available dye was blue. Brothers of all the orders wore skullcaps or broad-brimmed hats of beaver, felt, or straw. These hats, as pictured below, were sometimes decorated with a narrow band around the crown and tassels made of beads, seeds, or tiny seashells.

Fig. 16

Fig. 17

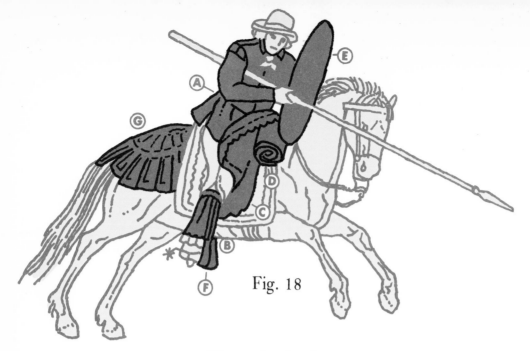

Fig. 18

The task of tying a vast wilderness together with only a thin string of presidios fell to the Spanish Army. With it came the deadly game of Indian fighting — days of riding through desert brush and cactus and a few sudden seconds of savage hit-and-run skirmishing.

Cloth heavy enough to stop an arrow was quickly shredded by thorns and rocks. The frontier soldiers of the 1700's took a cue from their conquistador great-granddaddies: they chose leather to protect themselves and their horses.

Figure 18, from a 1794 drawing, shows a *soldado de cuera* — leather-jacket soldier — of the presidio of Monterey, California. He is wearing the famous *cuera* (A), knee-length sleeveless jacket made of six to eight layers of well-cured deer- or cowhide fastened at the edges with strong seams. His lower legs are wrapped in deerskin *botas de campaña* (B) bell-shaped leggings — held just below the knees by thongs or ribbons. Protective leather skirts (C), called *armas*, hang from the pommel of the saddle. His cloak or blanketlike sarape (D) is rolled and fastened in front of the saddle. The oval shield (E), or *rodela*, was made of several layers of thick, rock-hard rawhide, stitched or riveted together. Flaps of leather (F) called tapaderos are fastened to each stirrup to shield the slipperlike shoes. The horse is protected by a thick leather rump covering (G) called an *anquera*.

The soldiers' uniforms varied throughout the years. The dragoon in Figure 18 seems to be wearing the uniform described in 1772 Army regulations: short jacket, breeches, neckerchief, hat, shoes, and leggings.

Figure 20, from an 1803 drawing, shows a soldier wearing a waist-length *cuera* and carrying an extra long lance.

Figure 19, from an 1830 painting of a Mexican presidial soldier, pictures a high-collared military jacket, *armas*, and fringed leggings. The tall hat, however, may be a beaver, the popular civilian headgear of the day.

Fig. 19

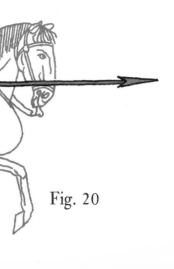

Fig. 20

29

The weapons of the leather-jacket soldiers were a blend of old and new. Their shields and eight-foot lances were unchanged from the days of Coronado. The narrow lance blade pictured below is twelve inches long and was uncovered at a presidio site in present-day Arizona. The inscription reads, "Presidio of Saint Ygnacio, Tubac."

By the 1700's, however, frontier soldiers had long since replaced harquebuses with reliable, lightweight, muzzle-loading carbines called escopetas. The Spanish type Miguelet flintlock and foot-shaped Catalan stock were popular.

Presidio Ꝑ Sᴺ,
YGNᵒ Tubac

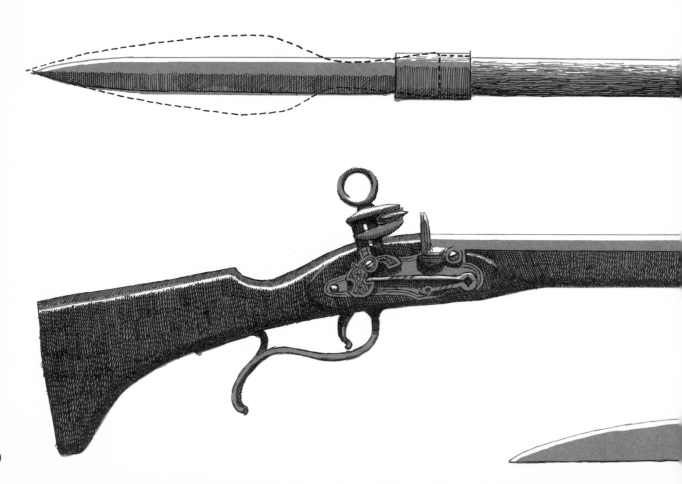

Although regulations called for heavy cavalry sabers, frontier troops preferred shorter *espadas anchas* — wide swords — not as much for weapons as for machetes to cut through tough desert brush.

On the wilderness frontiers troopers carried not only their arms and ammunition but water and food as well. Saddle trees of hardwood covered with rawhide were fitted with large, soft leather coverings called *mochilas* (see diagram, right). Field rations, sometimes little more than a handful of hard cornmeal biscuits and a mixture of ground corn, sugar, and spices, were carried in small bags attached to the *mochila*. Water was carried in hollowed gourds.

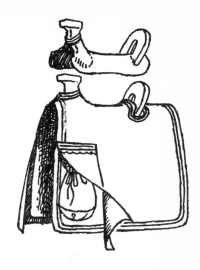

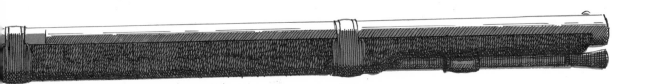

Above: Reconstruction of lance using head found in Tubac, Arizona. Many lance heads were wider, as indicated by dash lines, and had sockets for wooden poles.

Above: This favored escopeta has flintlock firing mechanism and 35-inch barrel.
Below: *Espada ancha* with 30-inch blade. Sheath for this handy sword was usually carried on left side of saddle.

31

A

B

In the 1770's, members of a small expedition on the frontier stop to question an Indian. Franciscan friar (A), wearing breeches and leggings under his habit, doffs straw hat to mop face. Equipment on offside of saddle (B) includes escopeta in fox skin case, water gourd, and shield. The dismounted soldier (C) has wide

C

buckskin shoulder band which holds black leather cartridge case. Band is stitched with name of soldier's presidio. Soldier's lance has leather grip and wrist strap.

D

Mounted soldier (D) adjusts *armas*. Horse equipment includes *reata* on saddle pommel attached to rawhide noseband. Handle of *espada ancha* is in front of rider's leg.

3. SPURS AND RIBBONS

Now the land belonged to the children of two worlds —
the blending of Spanish and Indian. The children looked
at their land, from the valleys of California to the rolling
plains of Texas, and saw a boundless range for countless
herds of cattle and horses. A village clustered about the thick-
walled church-fort. Square walls and square roofs challenged
the ancient oneness of earth and sky. Even the land was
squared into huge ranchos — so vast that boundaries were

marked not by fences but by rivers and mountains and the distance a man could see on a cloudless day.

By the 1750's men's dress in the Southwest frontier was beginning to take on a look of its own. The Spanish touches remained: broad-brimmed hats, brightly colored kerchiefs, waist sashes, and short jackets. However, knee-length breeches were left open at the bottom and the outer seams were often split several inches above the knees and decorated with silver or copper buttons. Frequently the seams and edges of the breeches and jackets were trimmed with satin.

Fig. 21

Velvet, velveteen, and corduroy of bright red, green, and blue were often used for jackets, with large buttons made from silver and gold coins. Breeches were made of the same material and lined along the inside of the legs with soft buckskin. A drawing in the previous chapter (Figure 18, page 28) shows a soldier wearing buckskin leggings of a simple wraparound design and breeches with the outside seam split above the knee. Figure 21, taken from a drawing by the same artist, shows an army sergeant wearing similar leggings, a military-style jacket, black hat, and neckerchief. The handsomely decorated sleeveless leather coat is a traveling garment rather than one of the bulky many-layered *cueras* used for armor.

Leggings were also worn by civilians. A list of clothing carried by the pioneer settlers of San Francisco in 1774 includes two pairs of buckskin *botas* per man.

At fiesta time workaday leggings were replaced with elaborate showpieces of fine leather, carved, embossed, colorfully lined, and caught up with fancy tasseled garters. Similarly, spurs were often worn more for show than use. A man could hardly walk while wearing a pair of extra-fancy spurs with huge four-inch rowels, such as pictured below. So well-to-do rancheros always had Indian lads waiting at the front doors of their homes to remove the spurs of guests.

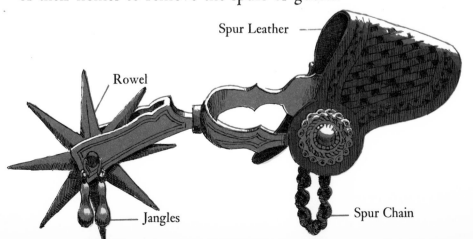

Spur Leather

Rowel

Jangles

Spur Chain

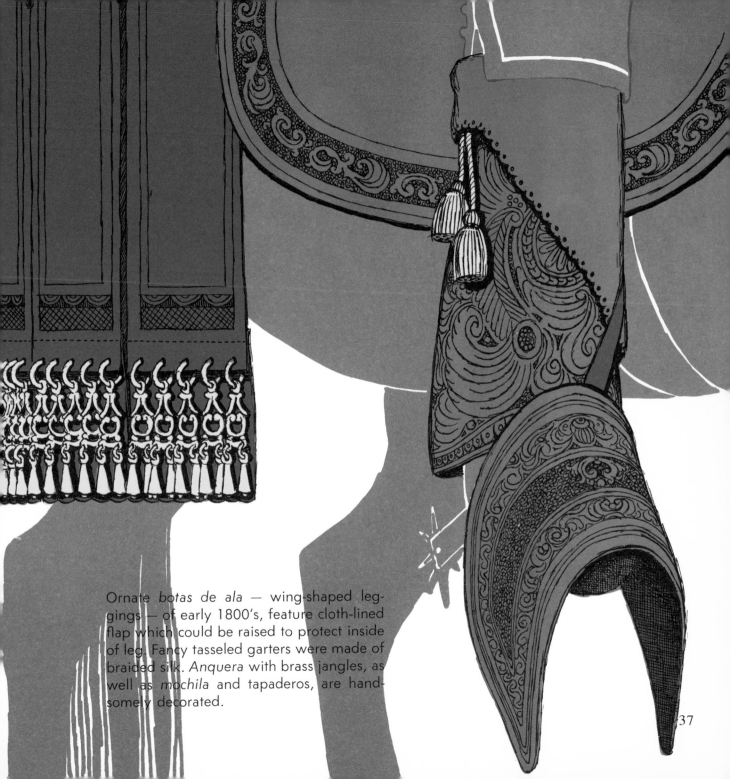

Ornate *botas de ala* — wing-shaped leggings — of early 1800's, feature cloth-lined flap which could be raised to protect inside of leg. Fancy tasseled garters were made of braided silk. *Anquera* with brass jangles, as well as *mochila* and tapaderos, are handsomely decorated.

Above: Basic woman's dress included loose-fitting cotton chemise (A), ruffled petticoat or under- skirt (B), bodice (C), skirt (D), and shawl or scarf (E).

Women's dress on the frontier changed little throughout the 1700's and early 1800's. Garments were hard to come by and usually worn until threadbare. A pair of decorated Moroccan leather slippers or a treasured silk neckerchief might be unpacked only during fiestas or holy days.

Figure 22, from a 1791 drawing of a wife of a California soldier, shows a typical costume: tight-waisted bodice with

Fig. 22

wide "U" neckline, three-quarter-length sleeves with ruffles at the end, and full skirt with ruffles at bottom. Sashes or kerchiefs were often tucked into the waist or tied around. Colorful silk kerchiefs were worn around the neck and shoulders, crossed over the breast, and pinned to the waist.

Fig. 23

The common headcovering was the *rebozo* (Figure 23, from an 1830 painting), made of cotton, silk, or lace, which could also be used as a scarf. Popular, too, was a colorfully embroidered and fringed shawl called *mantón de Manila* — shawl of Manila — which was brought from China aboard the Manila galleons.

Though delicate and expensive, lace mantillas were sometimes seen on the frontier. Figure 24, taken from a drawing of a fashionable Mexican lady of the 1830's, shows a white lace mantilla with one corner fastened to the hair just above the forehead and the rest falling over the shoulders and down the front. Women on horseback usually covered their heads with a *rebozo* or wore a hat.

Hairstyles varied. Unmarried women often parted their hair in the middle and let it fall loosely down the back. Married women usually wore their hair in two braids which they crossed and wound over the back of their head. Makeup was used sparingly. Perfume and scented powders were popular. Most women wore some kind of jewelry, especially necklaces and long, dangling earrings called *zarcillas largas*.

The famous carved and bejeweled high combs worn in the hair at the back of the head were seen in Southwest settlements, but not before the early 1800's.

Fig. 24

Fig. 25

The most common garment of the Southwest of the early 1800's was the famous sarape. Tightly woven of dyed wool, these colorful coverings measured about four feet by six feet. Some had a slit in the center for the head to pass through. Sarapes were especially suited to horse riders because they covered the arms, body, and legs and yet allowed the rider to move freely. They had other uses also — as a blanket, a pad, a pillow, or a poncho against rain. Some historians believe the sarape, which was first worn in the New World, came from a combination of the square cotton mantles worn by the Aztecs and the short capes of the Spanish conquistadores.

Below: Sarape of the famous Saltillo style, woven in a village of northern Mexico between late 1700's and early 1800's.

Figure 25, from a painting of the mid-1800's, shows a typical triangular pattern. A more ornate design appears in Figure 26, taken from a painting of about the same period. Figure 27, from an 1830 painting, pictures a *sarape de boca manga* of oval shape with a round center design and lined on the inside with contrasting material.

Another type of sarape with an opening for the head — called a *jorongo* — is the ancestor of the present-day poncho.

During this period, many wealthy rancheros preferred to wear a cloak of dark-blue or black broadcloth trimmed in velvet and ornamented with silver and gold thread.

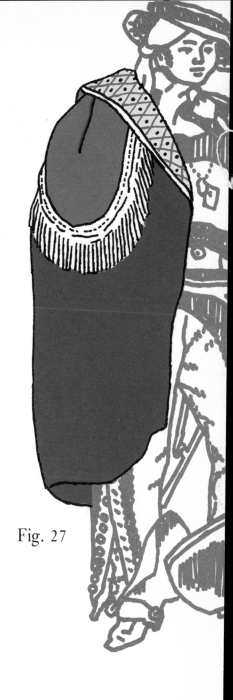

Fig. 27

Fig. 26

Fig. 28

Fig. 29

By the early 1800's long trousers had begun to replace knee-length breeches in European men's fashions. Styles in the Southwest changed as well, but very slowly. Many men continued to wear breeches — especially *vaqueros*, the hard-working cowboys of the huge cattle ranchos. Figure 28, from a drawing made in California in the mid-1800's, shows a *vaquero* wearing knee-length breeches and what appear to be *botas de ala*. The bottoms of his long white underdrawers — called *calzoncillos* — have been allowed to flare over the tops of his *botas* — a common style of the day.

The long trousers worn in the Southwest were far different from the close-fitting European models. They flared into a wide bell shape at the leg bottoms and were open along both outside seams from cuff to hip. This opening allowed room for the *botas*. It also gave the wearer some cool "air conditioning" against summer heat. Figure 29, from an 1830 lithograph, shows a Mexican shepherd wearing his trousers — or *calzoneras* — open to the knees. The legs of his white underdrawers almost touch the tops of his low-cut shoes.

A *vaquero* of the early 1800's, shown in Figure 30, wears his trousers open almost to the hip. But unlike the rider in Figure 28, this cowboy has stuffed the lower part of his underdrawers into the tops of his *botas*. He also wears the extra-short jacket which was popular among the *vaqueros*. These jackets, usually made of buckskin, were either plain workaday garments or handsomely decorated and velvet-trimmed showpieces, such as worn by the man pictured at the right.

This dashing *vaquero*, on his way to a gay fandango, carries his best sarape across his right shoulder, a bright-red kerchief on his head, and a shiny red satin sash around his waist. His long trousers of bright-blue velvet are handsomely trimmed, embroidered, and lined along the inside of the legs with buckskin. The split seams, held together by silver chains and balls, are open below the knees — just enough to show the bottoms of his snowy white underdrawers. A pair of black decorated deerskin slippers complete his wardrobe.

Fig. 30

43

A

B

Wealthy ranchero, his young daughter, and two *vaqueros* pause on their way to village in 1830's. Young lady (A) is dressed in holi-day finery. Most women were excellent riders despite difficult sidesaddle position. Equipment of *vaquero's* horse (B) includes wa-

C

D

terproof *armas para agua* of long-haired goatskin and decorated, seven paneled *anquera* with brass dangles. Rear view of *vaquero*

(C) shows method of securing waist sash. Ranchero (D) wears circular-style sarape, *botas de ala*, and huge, showy spurs.

On the frontier horsemanship was a way of life. Boys and girls rode almost before they could walk. An American sailor, visiting California in the 1830's, wrote that the men seemed always to be on horseback. And an ordinary piece of horse equipment was sometimes a work of art — whether an expensive silver ornamented saddle or a length of mecate rope, patiently woven of single strands of horsehair. Figure 31, taken from an 1830 drawing, is a case in point. The extra-fancy *armas* of this gallant *caballero* are made of elegant jaguar skin.

Leather was punched, stamped, carved, and often embroidered with hemp thread, as shown at the left. Wooden stirrups were common, some beautifully carved, as seen below, and covered with decorative tapaderos. Many different metals were used. The showy California-style bridle and bit pictured at the right includes a steel bit (A), copper "roller" (B), steel chains (C), and brass jangles (D). Ornaments and flashy cheek piece (E) were sometimes silver or gold. Lariat (F) was often braided rawhide. Mecate rope was used in decorative collar (G).

Fig. 31

Missions ⛪
Settlements 🏠
Indian Villages 🏠

42°   Boundary of 1819

Sn Francisco
Monterey
Sn Carlos
Sn Luis Obispo
Santa Barbara
Los Angeles
Sn Diego

← Portola-1769

Mogui
Acoma
Zuni
Santa Fe
Albuqueque

Tucson
Sn Xavier del Bac
Tubac
Altar
El Paso

Sn Saba
Sn Antonio de Valero
(The Alamo)
Sn Antonio de Bexar
Laredo

← Coronado-1540

Chihuahua

← Oñate-1598

Culiacan

La Paz

Mazatlan

In the early 1800's, three centuries after Coronado tramped into present-day Arizona, much of the Southwest was still a wilderness. Even the older settlements — San Antonio, Santa Fe, San Diego — were little more than outposts despite their 200-year history. But the people held onto a part of their elegant Spanish heritage — if only by the names they gave their settlements. One dusty little hamlet in Southern California was given a title fit for a European capital: the Village of Our Lady, Queen of the Angels. Today this frontier outpost has become a megalopolis. Unfortunately, its grand title

has been chopped to simply the Angels — better known as Los Angeles.

An equally musical title, La Bahía de Nuestra Señora del Rosario la Marinera — the Bay of Our Lady of the Rosary of the Sailors — has been shortened to Marin, the name of a county in Northern California.

Beautiful, too, was the name of a crumbling little church in Texas — La Misión de San Antonio de Valero — the Church of Saint Anthony of Valor. It is better remembered in history by a nickname — the Alamo.

4. CANNON AND CLOTH

First it was earth and sky. Now the adobe buildings and fences of ragged mesquite wood, the tiny gardens and dusty roads seemed as much a part of the land as the emptiness they replaced. Even the wind shared its song with bawling cattle, the strum of a guitar, the creak of an oxcart, and, from the east, the ugly sound of cannon. For the people of the East were as restless as they were proud. They behaved as if all the

land belonged to them. When they began to push westward, neither fierce Indians, tall mountains, nor boundaries drawn on maps were strong enough to stop them.

The early 1800's were topsy-turvy. New Spain broke its ties with Old World Spain and the Southwestern wilderness became part of a new country called Mexico. Only a few years later, settlers in the part of the frontier called Texas fought to break their ties with Mexico.

The rebellious settlers, among them such famous names as Davy Crockett and Jim Bowie, wore nondescript civilian garb — everything from fringed leather jackets and raccoon caps to fashionable frock coats and tall beaver hats.

Mexican soldiers marched to battle on a Texas frontier dressed in ornate uniforms copied from the French armies of Napoleon. The infantry soldier, pictured left, wears a tall, bell-shaped shako, frock coat, and long trousers. Mexican troops dressed like this stormed the walls of the Alamo side by side with barefoot farm boys conscripted as the army marched through Mexico.

Figure 32, taken from a painting of 1830, shows a mounted grenadier of the same period with French-style helmet boasting a bearskin crest. Horse equipment includes handsome jaguar skin covers for his saddle holsters.

A few years later settlers in California rose in revolt. Finally, in 1846, war was declared between Mexico and the

Fig. 32

Fig. 33

United States. All of the major battles were fought in Mexico. But when the U.S. "Army of the West" marched across the Southwest frontier, *los hijos del país* — the sons of the land — rode out to meet it. According to one American eyewitness, the rancheros went into battle dressed in Mexican costumes, wearing colorful sarapes and with gaily colored handkerchiefs fixed to their lances. Figure 33, from an on-the-spot drawing of a fight between U.S. troops and Californians, pictures costumes of both sides. The Mexican lancers are dressed in typical civilian garb — broad-brimmed hats, short jackets, and long trousers. Campaign dress for U.S. cavalry of the period included dark-blue forage caps, short dark-blue jackets with high collars, and light-blue trousers.

Figure 34, taken from a drawing by a U.S. sailor, shows a lancer wearing a military-style jacket. This Californian might have been a member of a local militia group.

Fig. 34

A

Mexican rancheros, U.S. cavalry-
man, and armed civilians meet on
Southwest frontier of 1846. Two
hijos del país (A, B) are armed
with escopeta and traditional

B

lance. Civilians in California revolt
included fur-trapping mountain
man (C) dressed in buckskin
trousers and beaded moccasins.
Lower portion of trousers has

C   D   E

been replaced with red flannel which dries faster when wet. U.S. Army dragoon (D) wears regulation uniform except for yellow band on forage cap. However, many soldiers replaced worn-out parts of uniforms with civilian garb picked up along the way. Settler (E) is dressed in frock coat, woolen shirt, trousers and boots.

The end of the Mexican War marked the end of three hundred years of Spanish and Mexican rule of the Southwest. A youthful United States now stretched from the Atlantic to the Pacific. But boundary lines on a map are one thing; a deeply rooted way of life is another. The Southwest — and the costumes of the people — changed very slowly. Figure 37, from a painting by a German artist who visited Texas in the mid-1800's, shows the costumes of a dancing couple. The man's short jacket and broad-brimmed hat and the lady's tight bodice and full ruffled skirt are familiar styles. But the artist's sharp eye had caught something new. The man is wearing leatherlike *chaparejos* — forerunners of American cowboys' famous chaps. Figure 38, taken from a painting by the same artist, shows a Texas *vaquero* wearing *chaparejos* on horseback. The fringed leather leggings worn by horse-riding American Indians from Texas to northern Montana were cut in much the same pattern.

Fig. 35

Fig. 36

Fig. 37

Fig. 38

Figure 35, taken from an 1850 drawing of a California *vaquero*, shows a familiar costume except that the traditional *botas* have been exchanged for Yankee boots. Figure 36, from an 1850 drawing of Texas rancheros, also shows no *botas*. However, other costume details, such as sarapes, sashes, and decorated jackets, date back forty years or more.

The shirt-sleeved California *vaquero*, shown in Figure 39, which was taken from a drawing made in the 1860's, has his legs protected by leather *armas* identical to those worn one hundred years before by famous *soldados de cuera*. And it is possible that a similar type of protection was used on a hot summer day some three centuries before, when Coronado's travel-weary cavalcade first made its way into the wilderness seeking golden dreams.

Fig. 39

GLOSSARY

Pronunciation guide for Spanish words and names which appear in the text.

adarga	(ah-*dahr*-gah)
adobe	(ah-*doh*-bay)
Alarcón, Hernando de	(ah-lahr-*cone*, air-*nahn*-do day)
anquera	(ahn-*kay*-rah)
armas	(*ahr*-mahs)
para agua	(*pah*-rah *ah*-wah)
bolero	(boy-*lay*-row)
botas de campaña	(*bow*-tahs day cahm-*pahn*-yah)
de ala	(day *ah*-lah)
caballero	(cah-bah-*yair*-row)
calzoncillos	(cahl-zone-*see*-yos)
calzoneras	(cahl-zone-*air*-ahs)
catalán	(cah-tah-*lahn*)
conquistador	(cone-kees-tah-*door*)
Coronado, Francisco Vázquez de	(core-oh-*nah*-do, frahn-*sees*-coh *bahs*-kays day)
cuera	(*kwair*-ah)
escopeta	(ays-coh-*pay*-tah)
espada ancha	(ays-*pah*-dah *ahn*-cha)
fandango	(fahn-*dahn*-go)
fiesta	(fee-*ace*-tah)
jorongo	(ho-*rohn*-go)

los hijos del país	(lohs *ee*-hohs dell *pay*-ees)
mantón de Manila	(mahn-*tone* day mahn-*ee*-lah)
mecate	(may-*cah*-tay)
Migulet	(mee-gway-*late*)
Oñate, Juan de	(ohn-*yah*-tay, wan day)
padre	(*pah*-dray)
presidio	(pray-see-*dee*-oh)
pueblo	(poo-*ay*-blow)
ranchero	(rahn-*chay*-row)
rancho	(*rahn*-cho)
rebozo	(ray-*bow*-zo)
rodela	(row-*day*-lah)
Saltillo	(sahl-*tee*-yoh)
sarape	(sah-*ra*-pay)
de boca manga	(day *bow*-cah *mahn*-gah)
soldado de cuera	(sol-*dah*-do day *kwair*-ah)
vaqueros	(bah-*kay*-rows)
zarcillas largas	(zahr-*see*-yahs *lahr*-gahs)

ILLUSTRATION CREDITS

Page 12, plate 1, New York Public Library.

Page 14, plate 2, American Museum of Natural History.

Page 29, Figure 19, Thomas Gilcrease Institute of American History and Art.

Page 41, Figure 26, History Division, Los Angeles County Museum of Natural History.

Page 43, Figure 30, Bancroft Library, University of California, Berkeley.

Some words of Spanish origin are still in common use in Western United States. English pronunciation varies according to regions.

adobe	building made from bricks of dried clay
bronco	(from *poto bronco*) half-tamed horse
buckaroo	(from *vaquero*) cowboy
chaps	(from *chaparejos*) protective leather leggings worn over a cowboy's trousers
corral	pen for horses or cattle
lariat	(from *la reata*) rope for catching horses or cattle
mustang	(from *mesteño*) wild horse, horse of mixed breed
ranch	(from *rancho*) place where cattle are raised, usually including rangeland
rodeo	public exhibition of cowboy skills

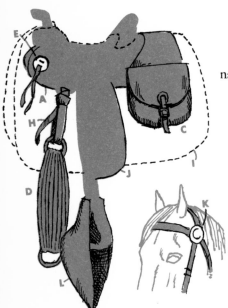

Diagram shows parts of present-day horse-riding equipment with Spanish names.

(A) *bastos*	(bah-stohs)
(B) bosal	(from *bozal* — bow-zahl)
(C) cantina	(cahn-tee-nah)
(D) cinch	(from *cincha* — seen-cha)
(E) conchas	(cone-chas)
(F) hackamore	(from *jáquima* — ha-kee-mah)
(G) honda	(hohn-dah)
(H) latigo	(lah-tee-go)
(I) mochila	(mow-chee-lah)
(J) rosaderos	(rose-ah-day-rose)
(K) rosettes	(rose-say-tays)
(L) tapadero	(tah-pah-day-row)

FLAGS OF THE SOUTHWEST

(A) Royal Flag of Spain
> White background, shield quartered by arms of Castile and León, topped by royal crown, surrounded by necklace of Order of the Golden Fleece

(B) National Flag of Mexico
> Vertical stripes of green, white, and red, Mexican coat of arms on white stripe

(C) Flag of the Republic of Texas, "Lone Star Flag"
> Vertical blue stripe with white star, horizontal white and red stripes

(D) Flag of the Republic of California, "Bear Flag"
> White background, brown star and bear, horizontal red stripe

(E) National Flag of the United States, 1846
> 28 stars on a field of blue, 13 horizontal red and white stripes

A

B

C

D

E

INDEX

The Author

GLEN DINES has written and/or illustrated well over a dozen children's books, most of them telling the history of the American frontiers. Mr. Dines attended the University of Washington in Seattle, the Art Center School in Los Angeles and received his B.A. and M.A. degrees from Sacramento College in California. He has executed many murals and illustrations for National Parks throughout the western states and Hawaii and has written historical articles for national magazines. Mr. Dines, a member of the Company of Military Historians and Collectors, lives in California.